Ma Barker and the Barker-Karpis Gang: The Controversial History of the Criminal Gang during the Great Depression

By Charles River Editors

Introduction

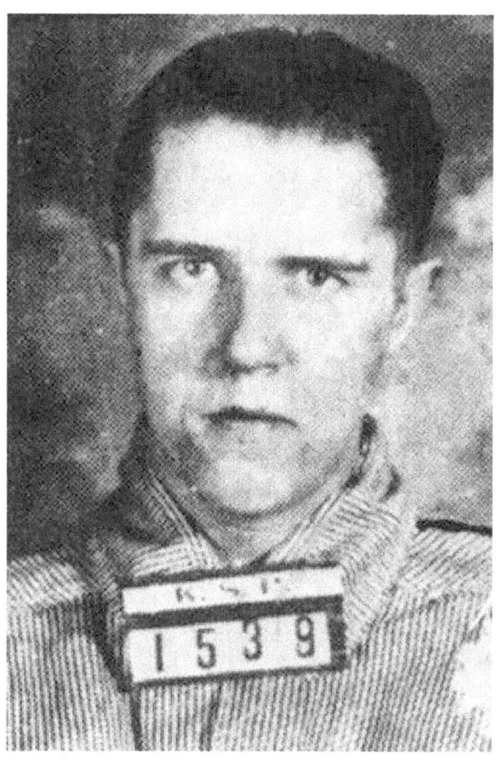

Alvin Karpis

America has always preferred heroes who weren't clean cut, an informal ode to the rugged individualism and pioneering spirit that defined the nation in previous centuries. The early 19th century saw the glorification of frontier folk heroes like Davy Crockett and Daniel Boone. After the Civil War, the outlaws of the West were more popular than the marshals, with Jesse James and Billy the Kid finding their way into dime novels. And at the height of the Great Depression in the 1930s, there were the "Public Enemies," common criminals and cold blooded murderers elevated to the level of folk heroes by a public frustrated with their own inability to make a living honestly.

Among America's most infamous "Public Enemies," perhaps the most unique and controversial was Kate Barker. With her prominent, hawk-tipped nose and plump, doughy face, framed by a classic dark curly coif and frilly day dresses to match, Ma Barker was as non-threatening as they come. Nary a second glance was given to this grandmotherly figure by those who crossed her path, perhaps at most a polite tip of the hat. Of course, as the age-old adage goes, appearances are often deceiving. According to the FBI and portrayals in popular culture, not only was Ma Barker a crass, greedy, and highly manipulative individual who coaxed her sons into the abyss-like vortex of criminality, she was the matriarchal mastermind of one of the most notorious gangs of the Dirty Thirties era.

The "Public Enemies Era," which coincided with the somber years of the Great Depression, produced some of the most renowned and ruthless gangs in all of American history. This was the era of the Dillinger Gang, a vicious company of ruffians whose collective rap sheet included at least 24 violent bank heists and four police station robberies. Meanwhile, other veteran bank robbers and career criminals, like Charles "Pretty Boy" Floyd, nicknamed "Robin Hood of the Cookson Hills" and branded "Public Enemy No. 1" in 1934, terrorized the Midwest. The public devoured the countless articles that their action-packed crimes generated with gusto, but few could compare to the meteoric whirlwind of morbid excitement that erupted when the sensational story of the Ma Barker Gang made its rounds.

The Ma Barker Gang, as they were so branded, wasn't a typical band of small-time crooks. Quite the contrary, the unorthodox family-run enterprise was, as described by FBI Director J. Edgar Hoover, "the most vicious, cold-blooded crew of murderers, kidnappers, and robbers in recent memory." The gang was as accomplished – and dangerous – as it was elusive, and between 1930 and 1933 alone, they made off with an estimated $3 million. In their heyday, the gang boasted some 25 members, and through it all, the Barker boys remained its core members. Blood, as per the Barker code, would always be thicker than water.

Of course, criminal gangs founded by blood brothers were nothing new. The Dalton Gang, which roamed the West in the late 19th century, was fronted by brothers Emmett, Robert, and Gratton Dalton. Another example can be found in the Shelton Brothers, captained by Carl, Earl, and Bernie Shelton, most known for the bloody territorial war they waged against the Birger Gang in the coal fields of southern Illinois during the early years of Prohibition.

The Ma Barker Gang, however, which was reportedly governed by the middle-aged, misleadingly unassuming, yet apparently ride-or-die mother of the Barker boys, easily warranted a class of its own. The obvious novelty of the alleged gang leader's identity aside, the disturbing fates of the Barker brothers and many of their associates served as a cautionary tale about the dangers and delusions that ensue when one becomes consumed by unbridled avarice and arrogance. But why were the Barker brothers, once innocent young lads, steered so far off the path of righteousness? What was the true depth of Ma's involvement in the gang's laundry list of despicable crimes? How did the once untouchable gang's winning streak culminate in such catastrophic disaster? The pursuit of the Barkers was a piece of what made the FBI a national institution, and alongside similar efforts to bring John Dillinger and Bonnie & Clyde to justice, the "G-Men" became the symbol of law and order in the early 1930s. The FBI's dissemination of information about Ma Barker all but cemented her notorious reputation, but in the decades since, FBI Director J. Edgar Hoover has become a controversial figure himself and modern historians have reached different conclusions about Ma Barker's involvement in the gang's criminal activities.

Alvin Karper, one of the gang's leaders, insisted, "The most ridiculous story in the annals of crime is that Ma Barker was the mastermind behind the Karpis-Barker gang…She wasn't a leader of criminals or even a criminal herself. There is not one police photograph of her or set of fingerprints taken while she was alive… she knew we were criminals but her participation in our careers was limited to one function: when we traveled together, we moved as a mother and her sons. What could look more innocent?"

Ma Barker and the Barker-Karpis Gang: The Controversial History of the Criminal Gang during the Great Depression chronicles the lives and crimes of the gang's members. Along with pictures depicting important people, places, and events, you will learn about Ma Barker and the gang like never before.

The Barkers

"She was the meanest cat

For she was really tough

She left her husband flat

He wasn't tough enough

She took her boys along

'Cause they were mean and strong..." – Boney M., "Ma Baker" (1977)

Ma Barker was born Arizona Donnie Clark in Ash Grove, Missouri on October 8, 1873. Known to her family simply as Arrie, she was the daughter of Emaline Parker and John Clark, a modest and unschooled farming couple of Scotch, Irish, and possibly Native American descent.

Other than that, however, the conditions that defined Ma's upbringing, like many other divisive aspects of the Barker Gang's history, remain a bone of contention. In some accounts, Ma's dismal, poverty-stricken childhood was further marred by the volatile temper of her abusive, alcoholic father and her God-fearing, submissive doormat of a mother. Ma presumably inherited her father's fiery wrath, while her combative nature, on the other hand, was compensation for her mother's excessive acquiescence.

Conversely, in other accounts, Ma's childhood was described as average and relatively uneventful. While the Clark family was by no means rich, they were not completely penniless either and more or less scraped by. Indeed, at one point, they were able to afford fiddle lessons for their daughter, as well as the occasional hayride.

Whatever the case, young Arrie always yearned for more, and her ambitions of one day living a life marked by comfort and luxury eventually morphed into an unhealthy obsession. Legend has it that Ma's thirst for boundless material wealth was further fueled by her fondness of cheap crime novelettes, particularly those that glamorized the dark adventures of Jesse James, the Dalton Gang, and other outlaws of the Wild West. When eight-year-old Arrie learned that the James-Younger Gang would be passing through Carthage, Missouri in the spring of 1881, she allegedly headed out the front door at once and hiked all the way to Jasper County, all for a glimpse of her beloved childhood hero. When the Dalton Gang, with the exception of Emmett Dalton, died at the hands of law enforcement and quick-thinking armed civilians during a foiled bank robbery in Coffeyville, Kansas in 1892, Ma mourned the fallen gang by donning an ink-black veil and dressing in dark-colored dresses for days on end.

Jesse James

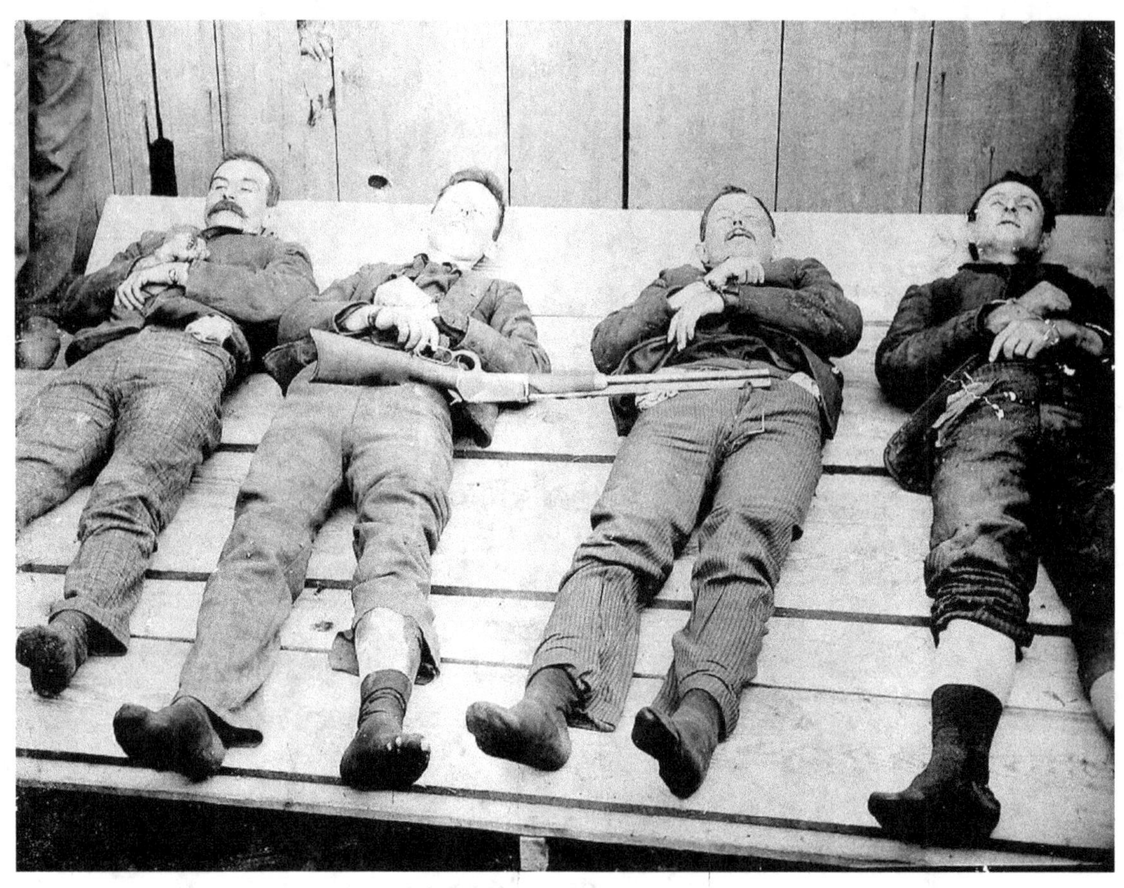

**A picture of dead Dalton Gang members after the
foiled robbery**

It was on September 4th of that same year that Ma, about
a month shy of her 19th birthday, exchanged vows with a
humble farmer named George Barker at a small chapel in
Lawrence County, Missouri. The newlyweds settled
nearby in the city of Aurora, and over the next decade
they had four boys: Herman, born in 1894; Lloyd, in
1896; Arthur, ("Doc") in 1899; and lastly, Fred, in 1902.
By the time of Fred's birth, Ma had retired her birth name,
Arizona, in favor of the name "Kate," and she had taken
her husband's surname.

Herman

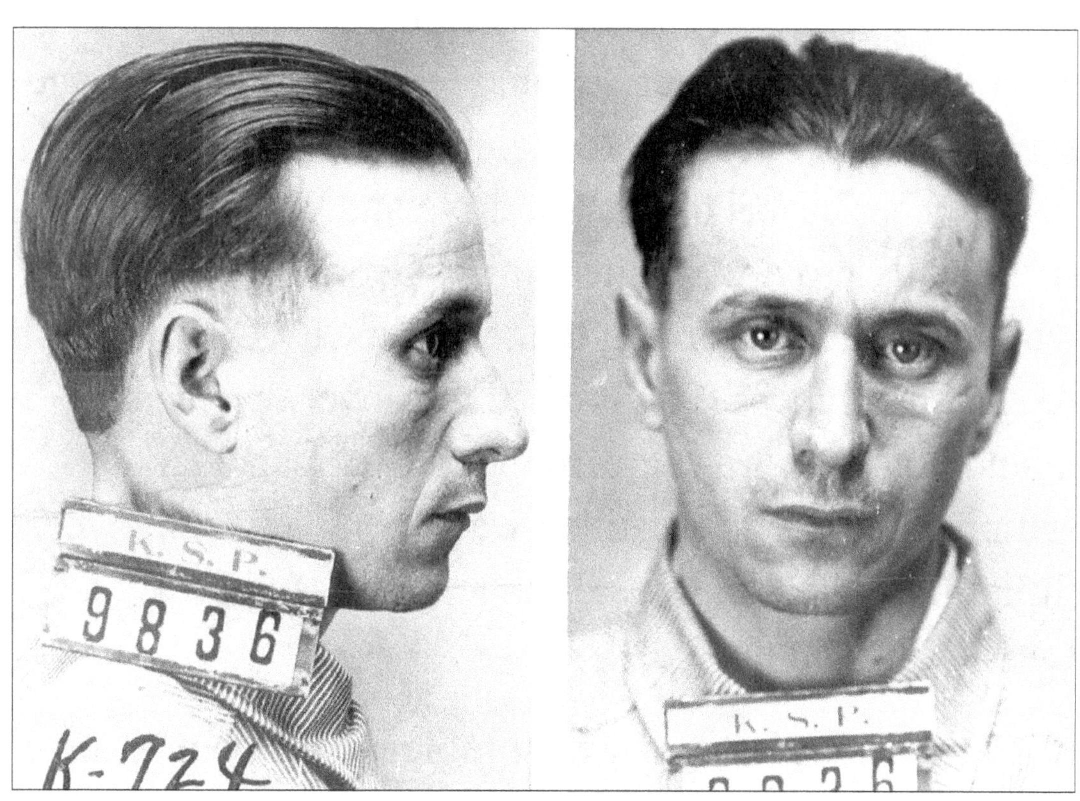

Fred

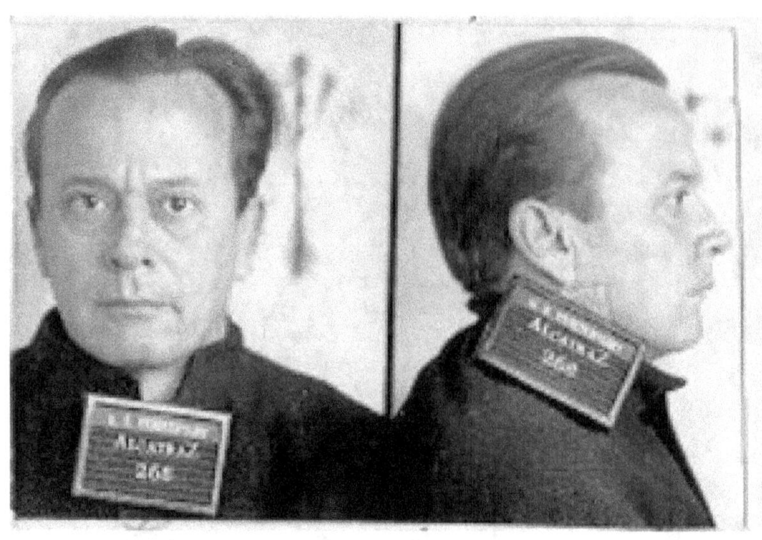

Doc

Ma's marriage was rocky from the start. She was, according to some biographers, an unaffectionate, overbearing, whiskey-chugging wife who regularly unleashed her ire on her dull and feeble-minded husband. It was no secret that Ma, though unemployed herself, resented her husband's lack of drive and his inability to sufficiently provide for the family. George had a solid work ethic, and according to the Tulsa City Directories, he juggled a number of low-skilled jobs over the years, including stints as a sharecropper, watchman, clerk, station engineer, and distilled water company employee. Still, the dinner table was often left bare, and bills frequently went unpaid.

Despite their glaring marital problems, the couple stayed together, at least for some time, and the Barker boys were Ma's pride and joy, for they potentially represented her ticket out of poverty. Although Ma rounded up her boys and marched them to Sunday Mass religiously, she showed no concern for their education and allowed their moral compasses to deteriorate, leaving the boys to skip class and wreak havoc in the neighborhood as they pleased. She even went so far as to encourage her boys to ditch school, and she supposedly spent the weekends, as well as the days they played hooky, educating them in the art of thievery.

The boys soon garnered a reputation as an unwashed and uncouth pack of rowdy miscreants who were only a notch or two above functional illiteracy, and they were detested by their classmates and neighbors alike. Whenever the delinquents made one of their rare appearances at school, the troublemakers picked on their peers relentlessly. They were described by one childhood acquaintance as "violent and unmerciful," and they instigated plenty of fights. Even so, Ma staunchly refused to remove her maternal blinkers, maintained that her sons could do no wrong, and aggressively challenged anyone who said otherwise. Time and time again, Ma retorted, "If the good people of this town don't like my boys, then the good people know what they can do!"

It did not take long for the Barkers' neighbors to grow weary of the brothers' vindictive antics and destructive shenanigans. They were finally driven out of Lawrence

County in 1904 or 1908 by the harried authorities and disgruntled citizens, who likened Ma's boys to the "sons of Satan." The Barkers collected what little belongings they had and relocated to Webb City, about 53 miles northwest of Aurora.

The Barker boys were granted a fresh slate, but no improvements were made in their conduct. If anything, the juvenile mischief perpetrated by the brothers continued to escalate, and they soon graduated from misguided troublemakers to full-fledged petty criminals. In 1910, Herman and Lloyd, then 16 and 14 respectively, founded a small youth gang of their own, marking an unofficial start to the Ma Barker Gang. The teenage thugs picked pockets, extorted money from defenseless shopkeepers, and used crowbars to break into boutiques, restaurants, and offices, and looted these establishments dry.

Even when the boys were caught red-handed, they received little more than a slap on the wrist, which they owed to Ma's theatrical performances and uncompromising bargaining sessions at the sheriff's office, as well as the corruption or incompetence of local law enforcement. Ma's manipulative arm-twisting skills were apparently so effective that she once convinced the authorities to drop the robbery charges leveled against Herman and talked them into releasing him into her custody, even after he had run over a child in his getaway car. Eventually, the authorities began to turn a blind eye to the Barker boys' crimes so as to spare themselves an encounter with their indefatigable defender.

Whether George approved of his sons' activities remains a matter of debate. FBI reports asserted that George had no qualms about his sons' misdeeds and profited from their spoils unstintingly, but there is little evidence to support this claim. In other accounts, George was an upstanding, but spineless individual who was appalled by the boys' misbehavior and exerted every effort to punish them, only to be thwarted by his wife, who reportedly berated him into submission.

Ma also took a proactive approach when it came to defending her boys by threatening to raise hell with those who dared sully their name. When Herman was accused of swiping the wallets of the deacons at their local church, she freshened up her curls, slipped on her finest Sunday dress, seized her son by the collar, and hauled him into the office of a Jasper County judge. She kicked off her performance with the struggling mother routine in the hopes of appealing to the judge's compassion. This was no more than a silly misunderstanding, she insisted - the boys were hyperactive, and at times they could "high-strung and mischievous," but deep down, they were good boys and were incapable of such wanton behavior, especially in the house of God. When the jaded judge showed no interest in entertaining her excuses, Ma puffed out her chest and cranked up the volume. The scowling mother shook her finger at the judge, demanded concrete proof, and launched into a strident tirade, accusing the authorities of incompetence and casting her sons as scapegoats. Naturally, the judge took great offense to these allegations, and when Ma realized that she had aggravated him, she turned on the waterworks. She apologized profusely on behalf of her son, and with a heaving chest and tear-stained cheeks, she implored the judge to withdraw the charges, just this once, and vowed to discipline him as soon as they returned home. Maddened by Ma's audacious and mercurial charade, the judge caved in and freed Herman.

  Ignorant to the concept of comeuppance, the Barker boys continued on with their crime sprees, which only worsened with time. In 1915, shortly after Herman was arrested yet again for grand theft auto, the family moved to Tulsa, Oklahoma, which had recently been crowned the "Oil Capital of the World." However, George's attempts to secure a steady, well-paying job were once more unsuccessful; he settled for a minimum-wage, labor-intensive post at the railroads, and the family of six continued to flounder in poverty, shacking up in a cramped, two-room cottage devoid of electricity and running water.

The Barker boys fancied themselves superior to low-income, but honest work, which they believed was reserved for chumps. Instead, they opted to profit from those who had and were continuing to profit from the oil boom. It was at this juncture that all the Barker boys, including 16-year-old Doc and 13-year-old Fred, began to fraternize with the hoodlums that loitered around Lincoln Forsythe School and the Central Park district. The young would-be gangsters christened themselves the "East Side Gang," also referred to as the "Central Park Gang," which was comprised of over 20 members in its prime. The Barker brothers developed solid friendships with members Harry Campbell, Volney "Curly" Davis, and William "Boxcar" Green, the former two of which would later become notable members of the Ma Barker Gang.

Ma remained fiercely supportive of her sons' dubious line of work, so much so that she converted their inconspicuous shanty into a safe haven for the boys' criminal associates and fugitive friends. She was, in essence, the "godmother" of the Central Park underworld. Crooks and felons would pussyfoot up to the Barkers' front door in the wee hours of the night, and they could expect to be fed, clothed, and sheltered. One such character who benefited from Ma's hospitality was a seasoned bank and train robber named Ethan "Al" Spencer, who later repaid Ma with a percentage of the $20,000 (roughly $380,000 today) he had plundered from a passenger train. The gang's ill-gotten gains, along with the spoils apportioned to Ma by her renegade house guests, fostered Ma's expensive tastes.

When Herman, Lloyd and a few other Central Park gang members were arrested in Joplin, Missouri and charged with "highway robbery" in early March that year, it was predictably Ma again who came to their rescue. "Lies, all lies!" Ma cried to their arresting officers. "You're lying [about] my boys!" A mountain of evidence was stacked up against them, including several eyewitness accounts, but the Joplin officers, who were unfamiliar with Ma's playbook, quickly folded and released them. High on his continuously swelling arrogance, Herman resumed his capers. For some time, he peddled scam subscriptions to a non-existent newspaper, casing the homes of unsuspecting customers, which the gang later burgled.

Come November, a clerk discovered Herman in the basement of Jackson Drugs, along with a satchel stuffed with burglary instruments. When Herman was charged with theft, Ma stormed into the police station where her son was being held and bailed him out yet again, but her tricks were growing stale. Herman was pinched again in Springfield on August 13, 1916 for helping himself to an assortment of watches, rings, buckles, stickpins, and other bejeweled ornaments from the Hawkins and Miller Jewelry store, and for that he received a four-year sentence. Evidently, Ma's masquerades did him no good this time, but the resourceful Herman teamed up with another inmate named Ed Conn and managed to lift three revolvers from the jailer's desk, which they used to bust out of prison.

Herman hitchhiked to Montana and remained on the lam for several months under the alias "Bert Lavender" until he was apprehended following a botched burglary and bussed back to prison. Doc, too, was caught dead to rights in early July 1918 and was subsequently charged with car theft by the Tulsa court. One by one, the authorities nabbed the Barker brothers, and for a while, it seemed as if their reign of terror was coming to a close.

Interestingly enough, unlike the rest of his brothers, who went on to become charter members of the Ma Barker Gang, Lloyd enlisted in the military in Tulsa roughly two months after Doc's arrest and was employed as a cook in the 162nd Despot Brigade until February 1919. Upon his discharge, he tried his hand at the straight and narrow path and worked a couple of odd jobs, but he ultimately failed to resist the siren call of crime. On June 17, 1921, Lloyd, along with Green and another accomplice, robbed a postal truck in Baxter Springs, Kansas and fled with $7,500 (approximately $85,600 today) in cash and bonds. Lloyd was charged with a federal crime, and in January 1922 he was sentenced to 25 years, to be served at Leavenworth Penitentiary. Never again would Ma see her second-born outside of prison.

Ma's heartache was compounded by the sentencing of her third son, Doc, on January 16. He was sentenced to a lifetime behind bars at the Oklahoma State Penitentiary for his involvement in a murder in August of the previous year. Doc and Davis had been emptying a safe in the ground-floor office of St. John's Hospital in Tulsa when a 74-year-old night watchman named Thomas Sherrill stumbled upon the scene. The bandits drew their pistols at the same time and fired one shot each. Doc's bullet struck Sherrill in the face, while Davis' was found lodged in his stomach.

Meanwhile, Herman, who had been released in the spring of 1921, breached his parole and established himself in Minnesota, where he proceeded to conduct another string of robberies. A few months later, Herman and a fellow paroled convict named Robert Egan broke into the offices of the John H. Ruge Jewelry Company and absconded with $4,000 worth of watches, diamonds, and gilded pocketknives from an unlocked safe. The pair purchased train tickets bound for Davenport, Iowa later that evening and made it all the way to the platform before they were waylaid by waiting policemen. Herman was escorted to the Minnesota State Penitentiary and was only unshackled in the summer of 1925.

On December 16, 1925, Herman, Fred, and two other accomplices descended upon an unnamed bank in Washington, Arkansas and took off with about $7,000. This particular heist was far from their best work. A flood of cops surrounded them upon their exit and a raucous shootout commenced, but Herman, Fred, and one of the other conspirators managed to slip away. A few days later, on December 19, Fred sauntered into the Central National Bank in Okmulgee, Oklahoma and, posing as "John Darrow," instructed a teller to convert multiple rolls of silver dollars, half-dollars, and 20-cent coins to paper notes. Smelling a rat, the teller sounded the alarm, but by the time the responding officers arrived, "Darrow" was long gone.

Herman and Fred continued on with the family business, and their exploits grew more and more erratic. This was encapsulated by the stunt they pulled on the outskirts of Tyro, Kansas on July 7, 1926. Herman and Fred were wandering around aimlessly on a country road when the elder Barker brother decided he was long overdue for a new set of wheels. The brothers soon happened upon the motor chariot of Charles Faurot, who was accompanied by his fiancée, Myrtle Rogers, in the passenger seat. The brothers waved their pistols at the startled driver and ordered the passengers to vacate the vehicle. When Faurot refused to comply, much to Myrtle's horror, Herman pulled the trigger and shot her fiancé dead.

Herman and Fred managed to evade prison for the murder and carjacking, but the latter was convicted of grand larceny for an unrelated incident on November 26 that year and received a 5-10 year sentence at Kansas State Prison.

With that, the eldest Barker brother was the only son left in the outside world.

A Gang Reborn

"Sons are the anchors of a mother's life." – attributed to Sophocles

With the Barker Gang mostly behind bars, Herman collaborated with the Kimes-Terrill Gang (also known as the "Terrill-Barker-Inman Gang") and embarked on another bank robbing spree in Oklahoma, Missouri, and Texas. The gang's trademark tactic, which consisted of attaching a safe to the bumper of a (usually stolen) truck via a winch and speeding off into the distance, was later adopted and occasionally utilized by the Barker Gang.

On August 1, 1927, Herman strolled into the America National Bank in Pine Bluffs, Wyoming with the intention of cashing $30 ($375 today) worth of traveler's checks, which he and some other accomplices had snatched from another bank in Buffalo, Kansas. The exchange would have been a cakewalk, but the teller that served him that day was no dupe. When the teller grilled Herman about the checks, he panicked and bolted from the scene. The cops were alerted, and a nearby officer, 45-year-old Deputy Sheriff Arthur Emil Osborn, gave chase. Herman and his wife (in some accounts, girlfriend), Mary Carol, who had been waiting for him in the car, were cornered in an alley some blocks away. As Osborn approached the driver's side of the car, Herman flashed his .32-Colt revolver and shot the deputy dead.

Herman struck again on August 9. At the stroke of midnight that evening, the Terrill-Barker-Inman Gang burst through the backdoor of the People's Bank in Southwest City, Missouri, but in the midst of the burglary, the thieves were confronted by the nightguard, William Hatfield. The thieves pounced on Hatfield and knocked him out cold, but rather than leave him be and flee, one of them shoved a shotgun in the stunned guard's mouth and blasted.

Herman appeared to have escaped scot-free yet again, and if it seems as if his fortunes were too good to be true, it is because that was precisely the case. On August 29, Herman and accomplices Porter Meek and Charles

Stalcup had just pilfered $200 (about $2,500 today) from the Newton Crystal Ice Plant and were en route to Wichita when they made a rookie mistake. Blanking out on the time, the outlaws careened down the streets and were quickly flagged down by Joseph Marshall and Frank Bush, a pair of motorcycle cops. Marshall peered into the vehicle, but before the cop could inquire for the driver's information, Herman yanked his head through the window, placed him in a chokehold, and pumped three .32-caliber bullets into his head. Bush, who stood just a few feet away, reacted swiftly and returned fire with several rounds, striking all three of his targets.

Meek and Stalcup, having both sustained bullet wounds to the legs, managed to limp away to safety before all hell broke loose. Herman had been hit square in the chest, and though the end was nigh, he would not go down without a fight. He slammed down on the gas pedal and zigzagged down the road until he plowed into a tree across from a 24-hour diner. Even at this point, Herman persistently crawled out the shattered window and hobbled across the street, and only then did he collapse. "Forgive me, Ma," Herman reportedly gurgled with his last breath. With that, he pressed his pistol up against his right temple and squeezed the trigger.

They say that the death of the eldest son was the straw that broke George's back. He was inconsolable, riddled with both grief and guilt, and with his remaining sons incarcerated, he fell into a depression and became little more than a hollow shell of a person. He stuck around for a couple of months and attempted to fulfill his husbandly duties, but he was unable to bear Ma's poisonous presence for much longer, and he eventually worked up the courage to leave Ma for good in early 1928. He wound up in Joplin, where he found work as a gas station attendant.

In some accounts, George's departure was involuntary. According to them, he was essentially kicked out of the house by his wife, who blamed him for their son's death and the family's misfortunes. Others suggested that George had inadvertently uncovered Ma's numerous sexual affairs with the neighbors and wanted nothing more to do with his philandering wife. In any case, Ma appeared to have been mostly unbothered by George's exit, but she elected to retain his surname and flipped her husband's absence to her advantage. Going forward, she began to play the part of bereaved widow and mother when it suited her.

Although George was now over 100 miles away from his wife and kids, he lived in constant fear for the rest of his life. He checked his windows and the locks on his doors obsessively before bed every night, frightened at the notion of his ex-wife or his sons tracking him down and snuffing him out for "knowing too much." As it later turned out, George's anxieties were not at all misplaced.

Meanwhile, in May 1930, a little under four years into Fred's sentence at the Kansas State Penitentiary in Lansing, he befriended a fellow inmate named Alvin "Old Creepy" Karpis, a practiced and highly intelligent 23-year-old career criminal blessed with a "near-perfect" photographic memory. Like the dysfunctional Barker boys, Karpis, who was born in Montreal, Canada to Lithuanian immigrant parents, was raised in an indigent household and was lured into the criminal world at an early age. He began hawking pornography shortly after his 10th birthday and was soon running errands for bootleggers, pimps, and gambling lords in Topeka, Kansas.

Moreover, like the Barker boys, Karpis was a devious, slippery character. Back in 1926, Karpis had been convicted of burglary charges and received a 10-year sentence at the State Industrial Reformatory in Hutchinson, Kansas. However, on March 9, 1929, Karpis and fellow prisoner Lawrence "Larry" DeVol, an expert safecracker, cop-killer, and future member of the Barker Gang, broke out of the facility and hitchhiked to Pueblo, Colorado. From there, they continued south. DeVol was nabbed five months later when the pair was in the midst of burglarizing a retail store in Woodward, Oklahoma and ended up back in the reformatory. Karpis remained on the run for over a year before he was captured and transferred back to Kansas State Penitentiary.

DeVol

Given their similar upbringings and rap sheets, as well as their complementary heist-planning methods, Fred and Karpis clicked at once. They pledged to partner up as soon as they both got loose, and as a result, the Ma Barker Gang, alternatively referred to as the "Barker-Karpis Gang," was revived. The duo spent the remaining days of their sentences sharing nostalgic stories about past joyrides, swindles, and stings; exchanged tips and tricks; and mapped out their future schemes. They would start small to keep a low profile, limiting themselves to after-hours burglaries of retailers and other non-confrontational crimes. Only after they had firmly reestablished themselves with a sound hideaway and other reliable accomplices would they advance to daylight heists and the like.

In the meantime, Ma continued to grieve for Herman and her imprisoned sons, and she began to ache for companionship. She consorted and occasionally spent the night with a few men – possibly past paramours – and eventually entered a more serious, live-in relationship with a 69-year-old man named Arthur Dunlop. Unfortunately, it wasn't long before the sparks from their honeymoon phase fizzled out. Like George, Dunlop was a shortsighted, aimless underachiever, and worse yet, the latter was a jobless alcoholic who preferred to lounge around the house with her.

In short, Dunlop did little at best to fill the void, and lonelier than ever, Ma decided to take matters into her own hands. She strutted down to the Tulsa and Kansas courts, harassing the prison wardens and parole boards week after week, and made several unscheduled visits to the offices of the respective state governors, campaigning for clemency and the release of her sons. She wept, hurled insults, threatened the authorities, and offered handsome bribes without pause.

Finally, she wore them down. Fred was presented with his release forms in the spring of 1931, while Karpis managed to shave a substantial amount of time off his sentence by fulfilling the quotas at the prison-owned coal mines. Ultimately, he went free on May 31, 1931.

Following his release, Karpis headed 168 miles south to Joplin, where Fred, who was temporarily boarding with Jimmie Creighton, awaited him. Creighton was another hardened, all-around career crook with a history of robbery, kidnapping, and attempted murder who had previously worked with DeVol, who himself had been paroled in the end of 1929; Creighton and DeVol were the perpetrators of the double murder of two businessmen at the Hotel Severs in Muskogee just a month before Karpis' release.

On the evening of Fred and Karpis' reunion, Fred contacted Ma and Herman's widow, Carol, by telegram and intimated their plans. He instructed his mother to sit tight and assured her that he would be back home with her in no time, after the matter of "procuring funds" had been dealt with.

The newly-paroled duo returned to work, so to speak, on June 10, but to their chagrin, they were much rustier than they had anticipated. Fred, Karpis (who had adopted the alias "George Haller"), and two other accomplices – identified as Joe Howard and Sam Coker – broke into a jewelry boutique in Tulsa and were in the process of smashing the glass display cases when they were found by some beat cops. Fred was convicted of this crime and charged for a separate burglary, so he spent some time in a prison in Claremore before participating in a mass breakout on August 16. His partner-in-crime Karpis was tried in the city of Henryetta and initially given a four-year sentence, but it was commuted to time served on September 11 when he entered a guilty plea and returned the stolen merchandise. Howard posted bail shortly after his arrest and skipped town, never to be heard from again. Their other accomplice, Coker, wasn't as fortunate - the fugitive, who had previously escaped, was transported back to McAlester and forced to resume his 30-year sentence for bank robbery.

Upon his release, Karpis joined Fred and Ma at a remote, nondescript farm that had been rented under Dunlop's name and was situated on the fringes of Thayer, Missouri. The hidden farm was the perfect lair for those in their "profession." The safehouse's seclusion aside, the fences were topped with tangled knots of barbed wire, and an electric alarm bell had been hooked up to the front gate that notified its inhabitants of unplanned visitors and trespassers. As Fred had expected, Ma and Karpis got along swimmingly. In time, Ma came to regard Karpis as an adopted son of sorts.

Rather than dive back into the field, the gang took some time to regroup and recalibrate their strategies, hoping to avoid a repeat of the June 10th fiasco. It was during this time that they became acquainted with a former veteran-turned-outlaw named Phoenix Donald, more commonly known as "Bill 'Willie' Weaver." He had struck up a friendship with Doc and Davis during his time at Oklahoma State. He had been serving his sixth year of a life sentence for bank robbery and murder, but he was paroled 10 days after Fred and Karpis' arrests and had coincidentally moved into his sister's farm just two miles away from Dunlop's residence. Weaver was precisely the type of man they were looking for, and he was soon invited to join the crew, which he gladly accepted. On October 7, Fred, Karpis, Weaver, and another bandit named Jimmie Wilson set upon the People's Bank in the city of Mountain View, Howell County, and they made off with $14,000 (approximately $201,700 today) in cash and bonds.

The serial jailbirds had had enough of the slammer, and from then on they would grant no mercy to anyone who possibly stood in their way. Back on September 2, nine days before Karpis was paroled, Fred and another accomplice forced their way into the Hildrith Chevrolet dealership in Monett with the objective of stealing a ride for the upcoming bank job. A 45-year-old nightguard, Elisha Hagler, raced to the scene to investigate the commotion and came face-to-face with the thieves.

Without so much as a second thought, Fred reached for his pistol and blasted away. One of the bullets penetrated Hagler's back and ripped through his spine, killing him instantly.

  The gang found themselves in a similar predicament on November 8. Fred, Karpis, and Weaver were reconnoitering a bank in Pocahontas, Arkansas when the town's chief nightwatchman, Manley Jackson, happened upon the scene. Jackson ducked into the shadows and began jotting down the license plate number of their parked car, but unfortunately he was soon spotted by Fred, who quickly subdued him and shepherded him into the car with his .45-revolver. The trio then drove the unarmed Jackson into a dimly lit quarry and disposed of his corpse, which was peppered with bullets.

  One of the most high-profile episodes in the early years of the renewed gang's career unfolded on December 19, 1931. Fred and Karpis had targeted the upscale McCallon's Clothing Store in West Plains, Missouri the previous evening and had made off with $2,000 worth of high-priced couture. The duo's discretion, however, left much to be desired. The authorities received multiple calls from civilians who had seen two suspicious-looking individuals lingering in the vicinity within the timeframe, and the suspects' car was identified as a stolen blue 1931 DeSoto. The local newspapers reported on the break-in and burglary on the morning of the 19th, and the reports included descriptions of the suspects at large.

Seemingly oblivious to the publication of these articles, Fred, Karpis, and a third individual – a young college student named J. Gross who had thumbed them down for a ride – pulled in to Davidson Motor Garage and requested that the workers repair two flat tires. The mechanic recognized the model of the stolen vehicle immediately, and a second red flag was raised when he caught sight of the stolen merchandise in the backseat. The mechanic subtly notified his employer, who in turn, rang up the Howell County police in his office and relayed the information to Sheriff C. Roy Kelly.

Sheriff Kelly arrived at the garage with the proprietor of the burgled establishment, Clarence McCallon, about 20 minutes later, just as the trio was backing out of the garage. Kelly disembarked from his police car and, with his service gun in hand, cautiously approached the driver's side of the DeSoto. The DeSoto's occupants opened fire at once. Four .38-caliber bullets from Karpis' gun punched through Kelly's chest and two bullets from Fred's .45-pistol struck his right arm. The pair, deciding it best to shed the dead weight, thrust Gross out of the car and hightailed it out of there. The trembling and utterly traumatized hitchhiker was later brought in for questioning, but he was soon after released when it dawned on the authorities that he had simply been in the wrong place at the wrong time.

The coldblooded murder of the well-respected sheriff in broad daylight shook the town to its core. West Plains Police Chief James Bridges and Sheriff Lula Kelly, who inherited the post of her deceased husband, were resolved to dispense the justice that the townspeople so vigorously demanded, so a $1,200 ($17,300 today) reward was posted for the capture of the fugitives, along with their accomplices. Those with information regarding the whereabouts of Fred and Karpis would be rewarded $500 for each fugitive, and $100 was offered to those who could pinpoint the location of Dunlop and "Old Lady Arrie Barker." This was the first and last time that Ma was officially implicated by name in the gang's activities.

The authorities swooped down on they spacious four-room cottage on Dunlop's farm days later. They managed to retrieve the bulk of the stolen merchandise and found a number of photographs, identification papers, personal letters, and even a set of blueprints for the First National Bank in West Plains. The wanted men (and woman) themselves, on the contrary, were nowhere to be found.

Unbeknownst to the authorities, the fugitives had sought refuge at a chicken farm in Joplin belonging to Herbert Farmer. Farmer's foxhole was another lesser-known sanctuary that was regularly occupied by Midwestern outlaws, including the notorious Pretty Boy Floyd at one point. The outlaws recuperated here for a spell before they proceeded to St. Paul, Minnesota, as advised by Farmer, and upon their arrival they made a beeline for the Green Lantern Saloon on Wabasha Street. The speakeasy, stocked with barrels of illicit moonshine and tasty fried pork sandwiches, was a front for a well-connected bootlegger named Harry Sawyer, and it also served as a hideaway for runaway convicts.

The four of them weren't the only ones dodging the police. They were soon joined by Weaver, who feared that he would be incriminated in Sheriff Kelly's murder because his fellow gang members had dumped DeSoto near his sister's farm in Thayer. Furthermore, in the following months, they were reunited with two other familiar faces. The first was DeVol, who was wanted once again for the burglary of the Orpheum Theater and the shooting death of a police officer in Kirksville, Missouri two years prior. He was also suspected of being behind a number of other murders in Iowa, Nebraska, and Oklahoma. The second was Davis, who was granted a 20-month "leave of absence" from Oklahoma State in November later that year. He was scheduled to report back to the penitentiary on July 1, 1934, but as might have been expected, he failed to honor his promise. A month after Davis' release, he reconnected with his girlfriend, Edna Murray, also known as "Rabbits" and the "Kissing Bandit." Murray had just broken out of her cell via sawed-off bars with another prisoner, successfully completing her third escape from the Missouri State Penitentiary. Davis and Murray rekindled their romance, and soon after they traveled to St. Paul to join the Barker-Karpis Gang.

Fred, Ma, Karpis, and Dunlop bunked with Sawyer for a few days before they were directed to a new, more permanent hideout. They set up camp on 1031 South Robert Street, which they rented from a landlady named Helen Hannegraf, who lived next door. The foursome introduced themselves as the "Andersons" and posed as a family of traveling musicians. As the legend goes, the glossy violin cases they lugged around with them contained instruments of a different kind: Tommy guns.

Notwithstanding the bounties on their heads and the pressure of keeping up pretenses, Ma was living the high life. She loved their new home, a two-story duplex with a lace-white vinyl facade and a matching roof that was kitted out with a roomy, fully furnished parlor, interior kitchens, and multiple bedrooms and indoor baths. They had access to running water, electric lighting, and coal, which was used to heat up the interior. The icebox and pantry were always stocked with expensive cuts of steak and a variety of imported groceries. There was no shortage of brand-name dresses and duds in the Barkers' closets. They even rode around town in a glinting new ride: the latest Buick model, which they had purchased in full with cash.

   Contrary to what one would expect from fugitives, the "Andersons" were not recluses, nor were they the ill-mannered and unsociable neighbors that they were in their earlier years. Quite the opposite, the Andersons were described as a generous, amicable family who always greeted their neighbors with dazzling smiles and cheerful waves. They made appearances in neighborhood picnics, church socials, and other community events. Dunlop was often seen sharing a tumbler of whiskey with the landlady's son, Pete. In the same vein, the family was remembered as generous, bringing plenty of warm dishes to potlucks and granting unrequited favors to their neighbors. Ma Anderson's "sons" and "cousins" drove their landlady's granddaughter, Marian, to and from the local Catholic school on many occasions. Marian adored the Andersons, and in a later interview she insisted that they were "the nicest people." She recalled, "We'd hurry home from St. Matthew's [School] because if we got home early, we could walk Mrs. Barker's curly-haired [bulldog]. Whoever got there first, you'd get a nickel or a candy bar!"

   All the while, the gang's rapidly expanding roster reached new heights on New Year's Eve, 1931. Fred and Karpis were attending a New Year's Eve party hosted by Sawyer at the Green Lantern, and in the process they forged friendships with a number of new members and future associates. There was "Smiling" Gus Winkler, an armed robber and freelance hitman who often ran with Al Capone, as well as Isadore Blumenfeld, nicknamed "Kid Cann," a Minneapolis-based mobster sometimes referred to as the "Original Teflon Don." The duo was also introduced to numerous other long-time bank robbers, including Tommy J. Holden and Francis Keating of the notorious Holden-Keating Gang, Harvey Bailey, Frank "Jelly" Nash, and "Big Homer" Wilson. Bernard Phillips, Verne Miller, Charles Fitzgerald, Harry Campbell, Russell Gibson, Elmer Farmer, and other graduates of the Holden-Keating crew rounded out the gang in later years.

Winkler

In the Barker-Karpis Gang, snitches received far more than stitches. On March 7, 1932, a prostitute named Sadie Carmacher and her friend, Margaret Perry, the lover of a local gangster, made the fatal mistake of contacting the police at the neighboring town of Cambridge. In the hopes of collecting the reward money, the ladies spilled the beans on the retail robbery that six members of the gang had executed the previous week, which netted the crew $3,000. It did not take long for the gang to catch wind of the informants' activities, and Carmacher and Perry's charred, bullet-ridden corpses were found in a burnt car registered under Karpis' name just days later after it had been abandoned in Balsam Lake, Wisconsin. No one – not even those they considered "family" – was exempt from this draconian policy.

On March 29, Fred, Karpis, DeVol, Holden, and Phillips targeted the Second Northwestern National Bank in Minneapolis. The large-scale operation involved the mass hostage-taking of 28 employees and customers. Luckily for all those involved, the bandits' plans went off without a hitch, and the hostages, albeit understandably unnerved, were left unscathed. The bandits loaded a total of $266,500 ($75,000 in bills, $6,500 in coins, and $185,000 in bonds), a staggering loot equivalent to more than $3 million today, into their stolen Lincoln and disappeared without a trace.

As it turned out, the gang's luck in St. Paul would soon run out. At around 1:00 a.m. on April 25, their landlady's other son, Nick Hannegraf, decided to unwind with the latest edition of the pulp magazine, *True Detective Mysteries*. Lo and behold, several pages of this particular issue were dedicated to the Barker-Karpis Gang, and the lengthy article came complete with mugshots. Nick sprang out of his chair with the rolled-up magazine in his fist, drove to his mother's house, and shook her till she stirred.

"Look," Nick choked out as he thumbed through the magazine for the bookmarked page. Helen switched on her bedside lamp and squinted at the photographs. Her face turned a ghostly white as she gasped, "Why, Nick, those are the boys next door!"

Thanks to the gang's deep-rooted connections, they managed to elude capture yet again. The Central Police Station had been notified as early as 2:00 a.m., but the arresting officers took their sweet time and only arrived at the rental property at 11:00 a.m. When they arrived, the place was a mess. Doors were wide open, indistinct voices from the babbling radio poured out of the kitchen, and next to the hearty, half-eaten breakfast on the dining table sat an untouched pot of coffee, still warm to the touch.

In addition to a fishing box, Ma's fur coat, and several pairs of Fred's designer loafers, the gang had also left behind a treasure trove of evidence linking them to previous crimes. There were a number of stolen dresses with their labels snipped off. A few feet away lay an unlocked suitcase filled with two pistol cleaners, a box of .380 automatic bullets, a dozen .45-automatic shells, and four .16-gauge shotgun shells. A $500 bond that had been purloined from the Farmers Savings Bank in Alden, Iowa was tucked underneath the parlor rug. The whereabouts of the "Andersons" themselves and their bulldog, however, could not be determined. The gang had reportedly been tipped off by either Inspector James Crumley or Police

Chief Tom Brown, both allegedly on Sawyer's payroll, ahead of time.

   It was a close call, but Fred, Ma, and Karpis were livid nonetheless. According to Karpis and the Barkers, it was then that they decided to part ways with the weakest link. Dunlop, they complained, was a good-for-nothing freeloader and far too chatty for their liking. As such, they chose to leave him in the lurch on some country road. The last time they saw Dunlop, they claimed, he mentioned something about heading for Chicago, but whatever the case, he never made it to the Windy City. Others believed the gang was unaware of the Hannegrafs' involvement in tipping off the cops and surmised that Dunlop had accidentally blown the whistle by blabbing to some strangers at a pub in one of his drunken stupors. Either way, the residents of Webster, Wisconsin discovered Dunlop's naked body by Lake Fremstadt the very next day. The county coroner later determined that Dunlop had been shot three times at point-blank range. Next to Dunlop's body was a limp lady's glove drenched in blood.

   After a few nights at different fleabag motels, Fred, Ma, and Karpis moved into an apartment building on 414 West 46th Terrace in Kansas City, Missouri. This time, Ma, who had assumed the moniker of "A. F. Hunter," posed as a widow who was traveling across the country with her two sons. Weeks later, DeVol joined them in Kansas and rented another room in the same building. Holden, Keating, Bailey, Phillips, and Nash followed suit, posting up in similar rooms about a block or two away.

On June 17, 1932, seven members of the gang set upon the Citizens National Bank in Fort Scott, Kansas and took off with $47,000. Later that day, a jewel thief and old friend of Fred's named Jess Doyle was freed from Kansas State and was welcomed to the gang with open arms. A hefty portion of their day's earnings was splurged on an extravagant dinner and booze bonanza to celebrate Doyle's liberation and induction.

It wouldn't take long for the festivities to die down. On July 7, police officers swarmed the Mission Hills Golf Club and arrested Holden, Keating, and Bailey in one fell swoop. Phillips, who was also there, was the only one who managed to escape. He scrambled into his car, booked it out of the golf course, and wasted no time in reporting the events to his colleagues.

The gang thanked Phillips for the information and acted accordingly, but his convenient escape raised more than a few skeptical brows. Many reckoned that it was Phillips who had clued the cops in on the arrested members' whereabouts, and their suspicions were only raised further when they learned of Phillips' past life as a policeman who went by the name of "Philip Courtney." The following year, Phillips, Nash, and Miller were dispatched to New York on a business trip, and the rogue cop was never seen again. According to testimony provided by George "Machine Gun" Kelly years after his disappearance, Phillips was bound and gagged, driven out to the Minnesota woods, and stabbed to death with ice picks. Nash and Miller then drove the corpse somewhere off the beaten path just outside St. Paul and buried it in a shallow pit sealed with quicklime.

  Ma, Fred, Karpis, and Nash left town a few hours after the golf club raid and rented an obscure cabin in the city of White Bear Lake in Ramsey County, Minnesota. Once they were settled in, Fred and Karpis arranged a meeting with a mob attorney from Tulsa named J. Earl Smith and commissioned him for Bailey's defense. The crooked attorney accepted the fat envelope of cash, and this greed and impudence would be the death of him. On the day of Bailey's trial, Smith never showed up. Attorney James Sheppard was appointed in his place, and Smith's bloodied corpse was found near the Indian Hills Country Club in Tulsa on August 16.

  By now, authorities had deprived the gang of some of its most prominent members, but Fred and Karpis remained undaunted. On July 26, 1932, Fred, Karpis, Doyle, DeVol, and a new member named Earl Christman, all sporting farmer apparel, stormed the Cloud County Bank in

Concordia, Kansas, and fled with $200,000 in bonds, as well as $20,000 in cash. They struck again on August 18, this time at the Second National Bank in Beloit, Wisconsin, and sped off with $50,000.

The news that Ma and Fred had long been waiting for finally arrived on September 10th. In a seemingly fortuitous twist of events, Democratic Governor "Alfalfa Bill" Murray granted Doc Barker his parole in Oklahoma. The decision, apparently spurred by Murray's prison reform campaigns, came with one stipulation: Doc was never to return to Oklahoma. Upon his release, Doc visited his father in Neosho, Missouri, and stayed with him for some time before locating and later joining Ma, Fred, and the rest of the gang at their hideout in White Bear Lake.

Murray

At last, the Barker Gang was complete.

Kidnappings and Funerals

With Doc back in the fold, the gang began to formulate plans for another major heist, eyeing the Third Northwestern National Bank in Minneapolis during the first week of December in 1932. By now, bank heists were most assuredly in the gang's wheelhouse, but a strange, gnawing feeling bothered Ma. She could not put her finger on it, but there was something not quite right about this particular operation. Karpis, as the story goes, agreed with Ma, but for whatever reason, Karpis and the rest of the gang went along with the plan anyway.

In hindsight, the felons should have listened to Ma, because on December 16, Fred, Doc, Karpis, Davis, Doyle, and Weaver burst through the entrance of the Third Northwestern and pointed their pistols and Tommy guns at the screeching tellers and patrons. As the gang was rifling through the main safe, one of the bandits who had been tasked with keeping tabs on the hostages – 10 employees and six patrons – became distracted, allowing one of the astute, cool-headed tellers to extend one of her legs and step on the foot trigger under her desk, activating the silent alarm.

Officers Leo Gorski and Ira Evans, who were just minutes away from clocking out for the day, were dispatched to the scene. As soon as the cops pulled up to the bank, DeVol, who was posted outside as a lookout, sprayed them down with his Tommy gun. Gorski, Evans, and a nearby civilian were killed, and with that, the gang darted out the door with $92,000 in securities and $22,000 in cash. They managed to make a clean escape, or so they thought.

The gang sped off from East Hennepin Avenue to the "amusement area" in Como Park about five miles northwest of the bank, where they had stashed another getaway car: a forgettable green Chevrolet sedan. It was just as well, because a stray bullet from one of the gang's pistols had punctured one of their tires and another had detached itself owing to all the sharp twists and turns, rolling off somewhere between Snelling Avenue and Larpenteur Avenue.

As the gang was unloading their loot and weapons from the busted Lincoln into the trunk of the sedan, a passing car slowed to a halt. Driving this car was 29-year-old Oscar Erickson, who was on the first day of his new job as a door-to-door Christmas wreath salesman, and in the backseat was his buddy, 22-year-old Arthur Zachman. Seeing the state of the Lincoln and deducing that the gentlemen were in need of some help, or perhaps hoping that the men may be in the market for a garland or two, Erickson poked his head out of his window. Fred, never one to mull things over, assumed the worst and assumed that the stranger was memorizing the license plate on the Lincoln. Before Erickson could disclose his intentions, Fred aimed his pistol at him and fired two rounds. Aghast, Zachman took the wheel and hastened to the hospital, but there was nothing that could be done. Erickson succumbed to his injuries hours later.

On December 18, two days after the Third Northwestern job, DeVol was laying low with another unnamed felon at the Anbee Arms Apartments on 928 Grand Avenue, St. Paul. While inebriated, DeVol stepped out for more cigarettes and booze, and upon his return he mistook another apartment for his own. Needless to say, the apartment's inhabitant, who was peering out from behind the safety chain, had no inkling who DeVol was and told him to hit the road. DeVol did not take to his tone, and in response he drew his revolver and waved it around menacingly. The man slammed the door shut and swiftly notified the police.

Failing to grasp the severity of the situation, DeVol drifted off and eventually located his apartment. The intoxicated scoundrel, however, neglected to shut the door. Officers Hammergren and Kast arrived moments later and let themselves in. The cops encountered DeVol's felon friend and questioned him about the drunken "man with the rod." DeVol was indeed hammered, his friend replied, but denied that he had any kind of weapon. Of course, when they entered the bedroom, they were greeted by a swaying DeVol, attired only in his underwear, his pistol drawn and at the ready.

In the end, the cops managed to wrestle the gun from his hands and hauled him back to the station, but prior to their departure, the cops sifted through DeVol's belongings for other weapons and chanced upon a stack of bonds worth $10,000, as well as $1,700 in crisp bills with the currency bands from Third Northwestern still intact. DeVol pleaded guilty to "shooting the two coppers" two days later, and for that he received a life sentence.

While DeVol contended that he was not the gunman responsible for Erickson's death, he refused to cough up any names and made peace with taking the rap for the crime. Still, the officers managed to extract one key piece of information. The cops had been pressing him for the address to the gang's headquarters. DeVol initially sent them on wild goose chases with two false addresses, but after several rounds of "severe questioning," the convict buckled and produced the address to the hideout of some lower-tier gang members. The authorities raided the apartment at 209 East 16th Street and arrested Leonard Hankins and Robert Newbern. DeVol's brother, Clarence, who was posing as "James Colton," was apprehended soon after.

On April 4, 1933, Fred, Doc, Karpis, Davis, Doyle, Nash, and two newer recruits named Earl Christman and Eddie Green ransacked a bank in Fairbury, Nebraska and prepared to split with over $150,000 in cash and securities. It was Sawyer who introduced Christman, a crackerjack conman and escapee from the Indiana State Penitentiary, and his girlfriend Helen Ferguson to Fred and Karpis the previous year. Green, who would later be inducted into the Dillinger Gang, was a professional "jug-marker," which was essentially a heist planner for hire.

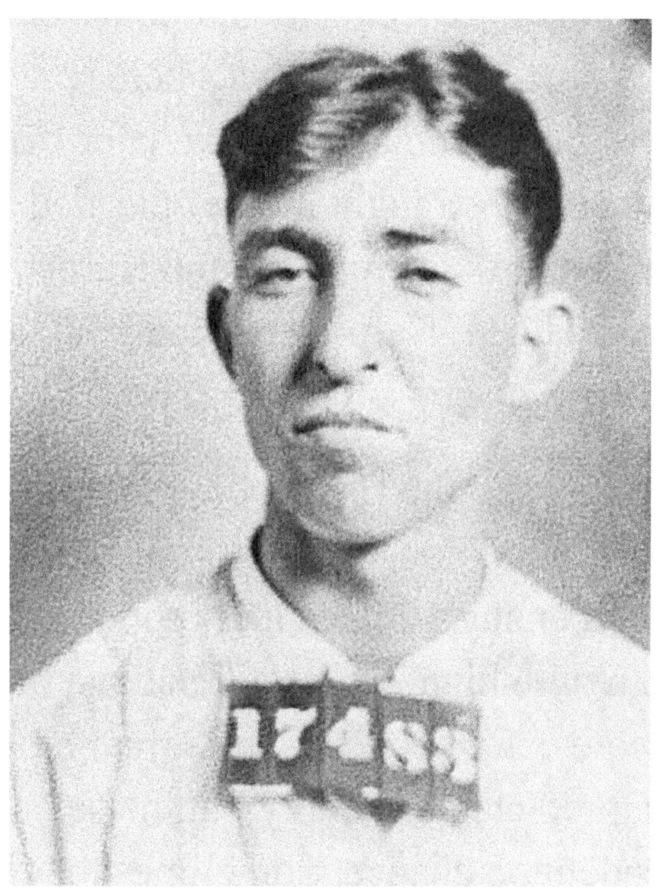

Green

Little did the gang know that the folks at Fairbury were not about to take this assault on their town lying down. Doyle and Fred were backing up the getaway cars, a black Buick and a navy-blue Chevrolet, when both the cops and armed civilians from the mushrooming crowd started shooting, and a messy gun battle ensued. Six civilians and one deputy sustained serious injuries. Christman was also shot in the gut.

The gang scattered handfuls of roofing nails behind them to impale the tires of those that attempted to follow them and hurried off to Miller's residence in Kansas City. There, they summoned a concierge doctor, but Christman could not be saved, and Christman's bereaved colleagues laid him to rest in an unmarked grave later that evening. When Christman's distraught mother pleaded for directions to her son's grave, Fred and Karpis, while sympathetic, declined. Karpis explained, "If she goes and digs up that stiff, the cops may hear about it."

By June, Karpis and the Barker boys were itching for a change of pace. Bank jobs and hold-ups were straightforward enough if executed properly, and they supplied them with high-octane adrenaline, but these operations were extremely stressful, often bloody, and incredibly unpredictable. Simply put, these paydays were far too dependent on chance. Sometimes they scored big, other times they settled for a thin sliver of the pie, and occasionally they got nothing at all. The loot they made off with from a Federal Reserve postal truck in Chicago, which resulted in the murder of Officer Miles Cunningham, consisted merely of canceled checks.

At this time, Fred and Doc were becoming increasingly concerned about Ma's welfare, as well as the possibility of her becoming a liability considering her age and declining health, which had impaired her mobility. They made the decision to move her into a comfortable and well-facilitated apartment on 114 Home Avenue in Oak Park, near the West Side of Chicago. They promised to call and visit as often as they could, and they reassured her that she would be in good hands. Christman's former moll, Ferguson, lived a stone's throw away, while Davis and Murray were hiding out at 219 North Second Avenue in Maywood, which was no more than an eight-minute drive.

After that, Karpis and the Barker brothers headed back to St. Paul, and it was there that they would find the change of pace that they had so pined for. One evening, an associate named Jack Peifer invited Fred, Doc, and Karpis to join him at the Hollyhocks speakeasy. The trio was introduced to Byron Bolton and Fred Goetz, also known as "Shotgun George" Ziegler. Goetz and Bolton were gangsters employed by Capone who were rumored to be involved in the St. Valentine's Day Massacre, and they were in the process of choreographing a kidnapping. As such, they were on the hunt for additional manpower and wanted to know if the gang would like to partake in the scheme. The gang happily accepted the proposal.

Thus, on June 15, Fred, Doc, Karpis, and Fitzgerald tagged along for the abduction of William Hamm, Jr. of the Theodore Hamm Brewing Company, all the while taking mental notes. The hostage had been blindfolded with goggles and a pillowcase before he was transported to a hideaway in Bensenville. Hamm was made to sign four carefully worded ransom letters that guaranteed his safety and freedom in return for $100,000. The letters included instructions for the dropoff. First, an intermediary was to drive up to a marked location on the highway by Pine City. Then, he was to wait for the signal – five blinks of the headlight – before setting the ransom money next to the road. The $100,000 was delivered a few days later, and Hamm was promptly released.

All in all, it seemed to be the slickest of smooth operations, and that might have been the case had it not been for the unveiling of a novel, but promising piece of technology known as "latent fingerprint identification," otherwise known as the "Silver Nitrate Method." A few months after the abduction, this method exposed the fingerprints of Doc, Karpis, and Fitzgerald smeared all over the ransom letters. This was, as an FBI-published article concluded, "the first time such a [technique] was used successfully to extract latent fingerprints from forensic evidence."

The day after Hamm was taken hostage, Nash was ambushed and arrested by federal agents in Hot Springs, Arkansas. Coincidentally, the doomed convict met his grisly end the day after, just hours before Hamm's release in an incident now remembered as the "Kansas City Massacre." Nash was being escorted back to Leavenworth and was brought to Union Station in Kansas for the transfer. There, Miller, Adam Richetti, and Pretty Boy Floyd emerged from the sidelines with machine guns in hand, ready to spring their compadre, but things went south fast. A federal agent and three other officers were killed in the frenzied shootout, and Nash was caught in the volley of gunfire and was struck in the head by a stray bullet. Miller's fate was similarly gruesome. Following the massacre, he endeavored to stay out of the public eye, but he was strangled with a clothesline and pummeled to death with a claw-hammer near Detroit in an unrelated altercation later that November.

On August 30, the gang returned to what they knew best and rode up to a post office in the southern district of St. Paul with a black sedan, which had been tricked out with a smoke machine and oil-slick devices. They swerved past the two police escorts, John Yeoman and Leo Pavlak, and made a lunge for the messengers, Herbert Cheyene and Joseph Hamilton, who had been charged with delivering the payroll for the Stockyards National Bank (in some accounts, for the Swift & Company food-processing firm). Both parties opened fire. Pavlak took a slug to the chest and bled out on the spot, while Yeoman, shot in the legs, was crippled for life. The gang fled with $33,000.

On the whole, it was a decent payday and would tide them over for some time, but again, it became apparent that the risks inflicted in such schemes outweighed the rewards. This compelled them to shake things up with a kidnapping of their own. Karpis and the Barker boys consulted Sawyer and Ziegler, and together they narrowed down their list of potential abductees before they settled upon 36-year-old Edward George Bremer, a scion of one of the most affluent and prestigious families in all of St. Paul. Bremer was president of the Commercial State Bank, heir to the Jason Schmidt Brewing Company, and the nephew of Otto Bremer, who chaired the American National Bank. It was believed to be Ziegler who submitted Bremer for consideration after coming across the family name in the papers after his father, Adolph, had donated a whopping $350,000 (roughly $6 million today) to the campaign of the Democratic presidential candidate, Franklin Roosevelt, in 1932. According to Edna Murray, however, it was Ma who offered up Bremer's name, and that they went with Bremer because they "always did what the ringleader Ma told them to."

At 8:25 sharp on January 17, 1934, Bremer dropped off his daughter Betty at the Summit School in St. Paul and headed for the bank, and as he waited for the red light on the corner of Lexington Parkway and Goodrich Avenue, Karpis popped up on the driver's side of Bremer's Lincoln and pushed him to the floor of the passenger's seat as Fred and Davis, who boxed him in from the opposite side of the vehicle, bashed him on the head with the butt of a .45-revolver. Bremer, unlike Hamm, was unwilling to go quietly; the plucky victim twisted and thrashed, and he managed to kick open the passenger door, but Davis swung the door shut, whacking him on the knee.

Once Bremer had been subdued, he was gagged and blindfolded with a pair of goggles, which they blacked out and secured with multiple layers of duct tape, and Karpis, who had slid into the driver's seat during the scuffle, floored it, with two other cars – one occupied by Fred and Davis, and the other by Weaver and Campbell – in tow. They pulled up to a deserted back road about 20 minutes away and ordered Bremer to sign three ransom notes, which bore instructions for his release. The ransom was set at $200,000, and should the Bremer family accept their terms, they were to purchase a two-line advertisement in the *Minneapolis Tribune* that simply read, "We are ready – Alice."

Bremer's Lincoln was abandoned at this location, and the hostage himself was transported to the gang's hideout in Bensenville, Illinois, where he was bound to a wooden chair in a drab, sparsely furnished room with boarded windows. Unlike Hamm, who remained unflustered throughout his "stay" and reportedly passed the time by participating in cooking sessions, poker games, and heart-to-hearts with his abductors, Bremer was a belligerent and ungrateful "house guest." He demanded booze, and he rejected the cup of coffee they prepared for him with contempt. He flailed and spat when they confiscated his wallet and ruby-encrusted gold watch. He called them crazy when they revealed the price of his freedom and was adamant that his family would never part with such an unreasonable sum.

Indeed, the incredibly high ransom demand and Bremer's name attracted a tide of attention from the press, to the extent that President Roosevelt himself personally signed on to lead the investigation. The explosive publicity spooked the gang, which is perhaps why they chose to spare Bremer's life, should the ransom be paid. Of course, while the media madness succeeded in raising awareness, it was in reality a double-edged sword because the authorities were inundated with bogus letters sent by pranksters and attention-seekers, resulting in the loss of precious time.

On February 16, 21 days after Bremer's abduction, the victim's family finally pooled together $115,000 in $10 notes and $85,000 in $5 bills, as instructed. Walter Magee, a family friend, was cast as intermediary. He drove to a pre-arranged location in the countryside, boarded another vehicle decorated in Shell Oil stickers, and shadowed a scheduled bus to Rochester. There, he rolled down a gravel path next to the hillside and approached the parked vehicle awaiting him. A flashlight was flashed five times, and, taking his cue, Magee set the briefcases next to the road and headed back to St. Paul. Bremer was untethered and dumped onto a back road in Rochester a little after 8:00 p.m. the following evening.

The ransom money was kept at the residence of Ziegler's uncle-in-law for a time before it was divvied up among the kidnappers, but rather than keep his head down, Ziegler, who was known in their circles as a pompous chatterbox, was apparently heard boasting about his involvement in the kidnapping to some mobsters in Chicago. He would pay dearly for his loose lips. On March 22, Ziegler popped in to the Minerva Tavern in Cicero for a bite to eat, and as soon as he exited the restaurant, a car sped past and a barrage of deafening gunshots filled the air. Ziegler, struck four times, slumped over and collapsed into the gutter. Some say that it was Ma who ordered the hit.

President Roosevelt made good on his word. The manhunt for the kidnappers, who had perpetrated "an attack on all we hold dear," was in full swing, and the kidnappers had underestimated the perceptiveness of their captive. Although Bremer's vision was entirely compromised, he was still able to provide concrete clues. He recalled that his captors had stopped for gas, and he even caught a glimpse of the wallpaper pattern in the room he was kept in.

Soon after, a farmer from Wisconsin came across a petrol canister that the gang had used in the stopover between Chicago and Minneapolis, and a dusting of the canister revealed Doc's fingerprints. The kidnappers' flashlights, which they had discarded at the drop-off spot, were retrieved days later and traced to a hardware store in St. Paul. The clerk fingered Karpis as the man who purchased those flashlights. Given these revelations, Doc, Fred, and Karpis went to the top of the Most Wanted list, and Ziegler, Gibson, Campbell, and Davis were also tied to the kidnapping.

The trio's mugshots were prominently featured in public service announcements in cinemas nationwide, as well as the 1934 spring issue of the *Liberty* magazine. Karpis later remembered, "It ran large pictures of Pretty Boy Floyd, Baby Face Nelson, Doc, Freddie, and me, and it offered a $5,000 reward to any man who brought us dead. The story called us 'mad dogs' and made a big point of underlining the fact that it would pay no reward if we were taken alive."

To say that the gang and their associates were on edge would be putting it lightly. Their contacts in Reno, who had previously laundered the ransom money from the

Hamm kidnapping in their casinos, refused to cooperate and severed ties with Bremer's abductors. The spoils were thus transferred to Chicago, but authorities soon sniffed out the illegitimate cash, and a number of conspirators, such as former state legislator John "Boss" McLaughlin, were apprehended.

Understandably, the gang thought it best to go their separate ways, at least for the time being. Doc and Karpis headed for Chicago, while Fred and Ma, accompanied by Campbell, traveled south to Ocklawaha, Florida and rented a cozy cottage by Lake Weir as the "Blackburns."

Despite these efforts, the gang's days were numbered.

The Final Showdown

When they broke ranks, the ringleaders had taken extra precautions to throw the cops off their scent. Sometime in March 1934, about a week before the gang split up, Fred and Karpis dropped by the office of Dr. Joseph Moran at the Irving Hotel in Chicago. Moran, the primary physician of the Chicago Outfit, was an old friend and co-conspirator who had aided the gang in laundering some of the ransom money through his practice. Moran received $1,250 in cash and began to prep for one of the greatest challenges of his questionable career. For Fred, he performed a round of back-alley rhinoplasty, and the agonizing pain he inflicted on the Barker brother was apparently so unbearable that the patient begged to be shot dead. In the end, Fred was left with several lasting scars, yet no visible changes were made to his appearance. Karpis' surgery, on the other hand, was a relative success. Moran sliced off the epidermis on Karpis' fingertips, soaked them in hydrochloric acid, and scraped off the pesky grooves with a scalpel.

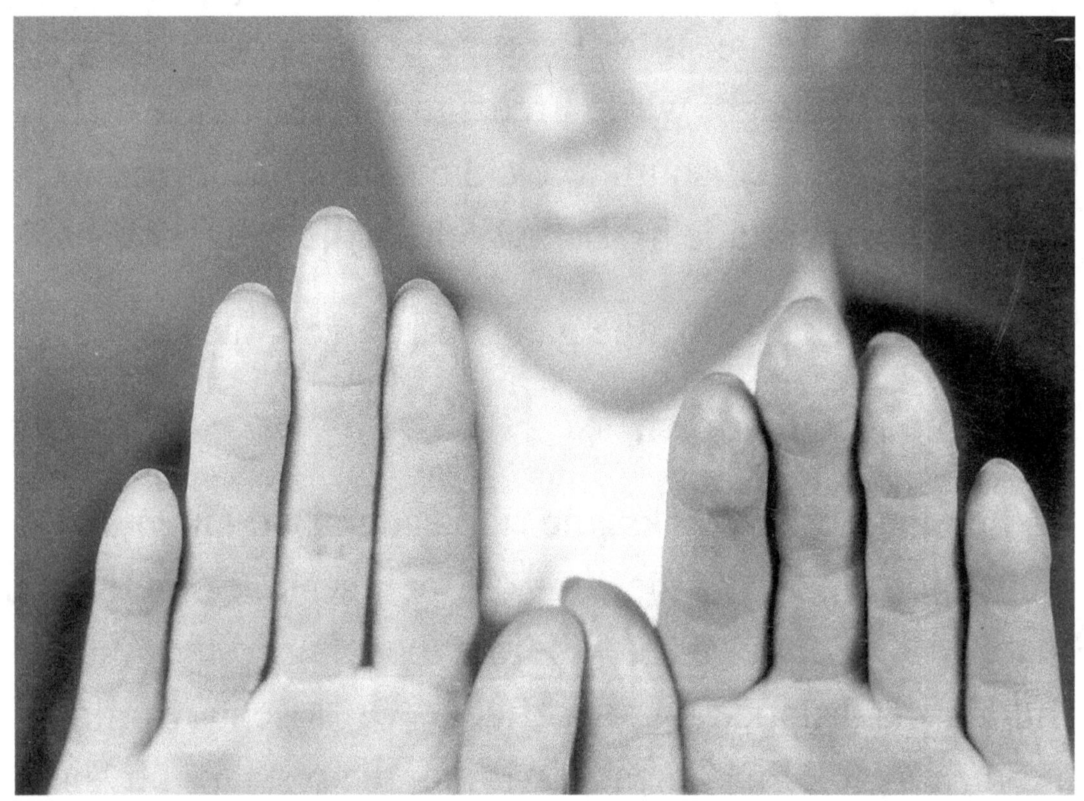

A picture of Karpis' altered fingertips

Like Dunlop and Ziegler, Moran did not know how to keep his mouth shut. He did not trumpet his exploits to anyone who would listen, but he made the critical mistake of threatening the gang members. Moran was knocking back a couple of drinks with some members of the gang in

Toledo about six months later, and in response to a jab at his character, he warned, "You better watch it. I have you guys in the palm of my hand." His rotting corpse was found along the Lake Erie shore without hands and feet, and his body was positively identified in July 1937. The circumstances surrounding his ghastly death remains unclear. Some say he was beaten to death for running his mouth, while others say he was doused in gasoline and set alight in retaliation for the excruciating pain Fred and Karpis suffered at his hands. While Karpis later claimed the body found on the shore wasn't Moran's, and that Fred and Doc killed Moran, it's widely accepted that Karpis and Fred took him for an ill-fated boat ride.

Either way, Moran was the least of the gang's mounting problems. In April, about a week or two after Fred's bungled surgery, FBI agents cornered jug-marker Eddie Green in St. Paul. Green sustained several bullet wounds in the head and shoulder, but he survived the assault and was taken to a nearby hospital. He managed to hold on for eight more days, and the federal agents observing him succeeded in obtaining significant clues from his deranged ranting and raving. Green's hysterical wife, Bessie, was also interrogated and produced more information in a bid to dissociate herself from the charges. It was Bessie who informed the feds that the Barker boys were on the run with their mother and thereby unintentionally planted the seeds for the legend of Ma Barker.

On the morning of January 8, 1935, Doc and his girlfriend, Mildren Kuhlman, were ambushed by a mob of federal agents outside of their apartment on 432 Surf Street. When the officers – among them Melvin Purvis, who had recently captured and killed Pretty Boy Floyd – searched Doc's apartment, they uncovered a map of Florida with the town of Ocklawaha encircled in red marker. Next to the map was a letter from Fred that mentioned a "palatial eight-room frame house with a houseboat" and recounted Fred's adventures in the little-known town, including the hunting of a beloved local icon, "Gator Joe."

Purvis

Hours later, agents descended upon another Barker Gang foxhole inhabited by Bolton, Gibson; Gibson's wife Clara, and Ruth Heidt, the widow of another recently killed gang member named William Harrison. Bolton, Clara, and Ruth were arrested without incident, but Gibson was another matter. He snatched up a .32-caliber revolver and an automatic and attempted to shimmy down the fire escape, only to be intercepted by a federal agent. While Doc remained devoted to his family and fellow gang members to the very end, Bolton, staring down the barrel of a lifetime sentence, was much more cooperative and confirmed the address of the hideout in Ocklawaha.

As a result, federal agent Earl Connelly and 14 of his colleagues arrived at the crack of dawn on January 16 and quietly positioned themselves around the Lake Weir cottage before making their presence known. Fred and Ma, who had been jolted awake from the sudden ruckus, were ordered to vacate the premises with their hands up.

The cottage

The officers, listening intently, could only decipher a couple of lines from the murmuring inside the cottage."What are you going to do?" the gravelly voice of an elderly woman inquired. Moments later, as if responding to her own question, she said, "Alright. Go ahead."

  Suddenly, a fusillade of roaring bullets erupted from within, spraying every which way. The shootout, punctuated by intermittent bursts of gunfire from both ends, dragged on for four suspenseful hours, during which the feds discharged anywhere between 1,500-2,000 rounds. After the longest shootout in the history of the FBI, Connelly waited another 45 minutes after the smoke had cleared before sending Willie Woodbury, a cook, housekeeper, handyman, and chauffeur employed by the Barkers, to gauge the status of the trigger-happy fugitives.

  Woodbury discovered that the 33-year-old gunman and his 61-year-old mother were dead. Fred was found in one of the bedrooms on the second floor with a body full of 14 bullets. Ma's motionless body, having been punctured by three bullets, was sprawled out just a few feet away. In addition to the Tommy guns reportedly found next to their bodies, the agents retrieved a number of unused bulletproof vests, two shotguns, a pair of .45 automatics, a Winchester rifle, another .380-automatic, several cases of ammunition, and a total of $14,293 in cash. Strangely enough, the weapons recovered at the crime scene were never dusted for prints, so it's unclear whether Ma Barker herself actively participated in the gun battle.

Newspapers across the country reported on the deaths of Fred and Ma Barker for weeks. Alongside these front-page articles was a black-and-white photograph of three federal agents striking a pose next to the deceased, displayed side-by-side with white sheets draped over their torsos. Fred and Ma remained in the local morgue until October that year, when George finally scrounged up the funds to collect their bodies and buried them next to Herman's grave. Months later, George filed for custody of the cash that had been seized from the crime scene, and his motion was ultimately granted because the authorities were unable to prove its source.

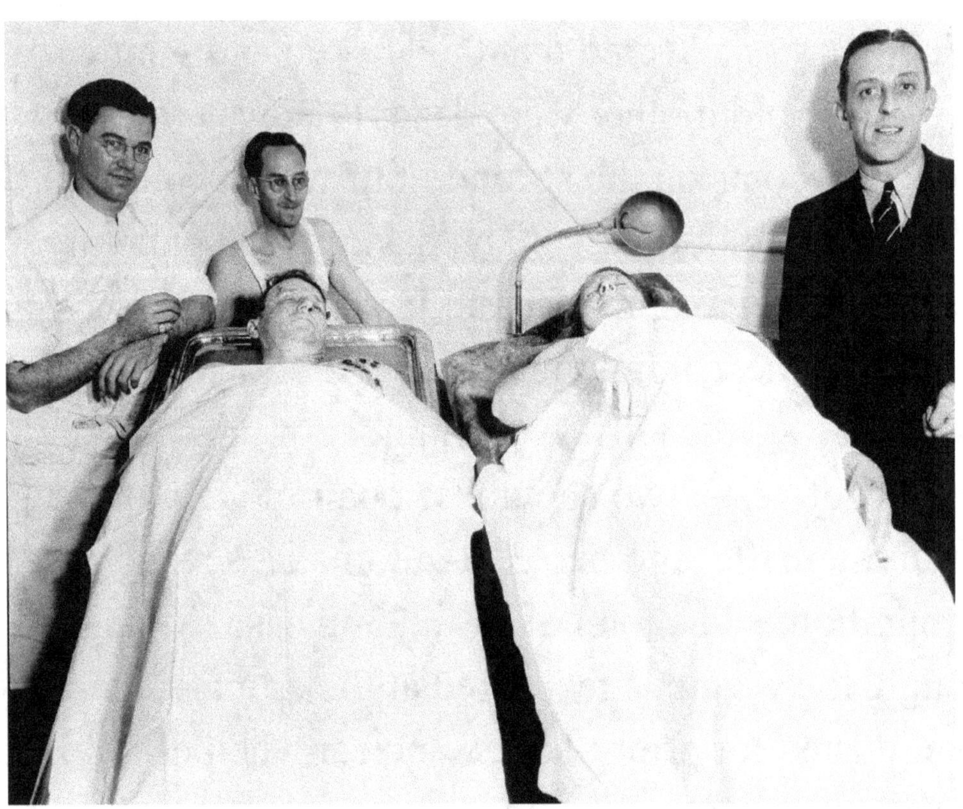

Karpis and Campbell decamped to Atlantic City immediately after they received word about the Lake Weir shootout. The pair, along with their girlfriends, Dolores Delaney and Wynona Burdette, were cornered at the Dan-Mor Hotel on January 20, and while Karpis and Campbell managed to evade capture following the ensuing struggle, and Delaney and Burdette weren't quite as lucky. Both women were arrested, convicted of harboring fugitives, and sentenced to five years.

Karpis and Campbell founded a new gang of their own in Ohio, where they executed a chain of mail robberies. Karpis continued to dodge the feds for over a year until he was apprehended by none other than J. Edgar Hoover himself in May 1936. Karpis was convicted of the Hamm kidnapping and spent the next 33 years of his life in different prisons, including Alcatraz. He was paroled in 1969 at the age of 62 and deported to Canada. He spent his final decade in Spain and penned two novels before dying of an overdose of sleeping pills on August 26, 1979.

Karpis was the only core member of the gang who lived long enough to enjoy his twilight years. Following his arrest, Doc was convicted of the Bremer kidnapping, and he was a given a life sentence, also to be served in Alcatraz. Ma Barker's only surviving son was among the first inmates at the new prison on the Rock, and as the men were being taken across the San Francisco Bay to their cells, rumors flew that the waters were infested with sharks.

D. Ramey Logan's picture of Alcatraz

Hoover in the 1930s

Alcatraz is the most notorious prison in American history for many reasons, one of which was the fact that it was the most secure. In fact, in the three decades it served as a prison, nearly three dozen prisoners tried to escape, which led to the "Battle of Alcatraz" and some of the most complex escape plans ever hatched to bust out, but nobody ever successfully escaped the Rock, and several died trying. As one commenter poignantly put it, "You break the rules, you go to prison. You break the prison rules, you go to Alcatraz Prison." Another writer echoed this sentiment, calling Alcatraz "the great garbage can of

San Francisco Bay, into which every federal prison dumped its most rotten apples."

Doc Barker was one of the first to learn this the hard way. On January 13, 1939, Doc vaulted over the prison walls and began to paddle away in his makeshift raft when he was struck twice by the guards' sniper rifles. He was brought to the prison hospital and treated for his injuries, but it was too late. "I'm all shot to hell," he uttered with his last breaths. "I was a fool to try it." He was interred at the Olivet Memorial Park Cemetery in Colma, California. There was no name on his homely tombstone, only his prison number: AZ-268.

Lloyd, as it turns out, was perhaps the least fortunate of all the Barker boys. He was paroled in late October 1938 and spent the remaining 11 years of his life as a contributing member of society, working for a time as a bartender and assistant manager at the Denargo Grill in Denver. At the time of his death, he was employed as the manager of the Denargo Market. He even served as an Army cook at a POW camp in Fort Custer, Michigan during World War II and was honorably discharged and awarded a medal for good conduct. The new life he built for himself – which was rounded out by a wife, Jennie Farrell, and four kids, two of which were from Farrell's previous marriage – came crashing down on March 18, 1949. That afternoon, Lloyd left work early and returned home to check on his ill wife, only to be shot in the head by her very own shotgun. Farrell, who was supposedly suffering from delusions and severe postpartum depression, was arrested and later sent to the Colorado State Insane Asylum.

In the end, the extent of Ma Barker's involvement in the gang's crimes has yet to be conclusively determined. Hoover himself called her "a monument...of parental indulgence" who was unable to rein in her ill-disciplined, destructive sons, and the FBI considered her a monstrous, murderous mother, "a mean, vicious beast of prey" and a "she-wolf" who "ruled [the gang] like a queen." That's generally how she's remembered today, and she's been portrayed like that ever since.

Conversely, those close to Kate Barker claimed she did not have a single criminal bone in her body and accused the feds of fabricating the allegations to justify their accidental shooting of the Barker matriarch. Woodbury, who had discovered her body, said in an interview years later, "I couldn't believe Ma had done all those things they said she did. She was better to me than my own Mama." Bailey echoed that sentiment in his autobiography, claiming Ma "couldn't even plan breakfast," let alone a full-fledged bank heist.

Karpis, one of the central figures in the drama, maintained to his death that Ma Barker was essentially uninvolved in the gang's criminal activities: "Ma...was somebody we looked after and took with us when we moved...hideout to hideout. It is no insult to Ma's memory that she just didn't have the know-how to direct us on a robbery. It would not have occurred to her to get involved in our business, and we always made it a point of only discussing our scores when Ma wasn't around. We'd leave her at home when we were arranging a jog, or we'd send her to a movie. Ma saw a lot of movies."

And thus, the mystery of Ma Barker, the most famous of them all, lives on.

Online Resources

Other books about 20th century American history by Charles River Editors

Other books about Ma Barker on Amazon

Further Reading

Bergerson, R. (2013, December 16). 1932 bank robbery ends with Christmas tragedy. Retrieved May 18, 2020, from https://www.parkbugle.org/1932-bank-robbery-ends-with-christmas-tragedy/

Brooks, J. (2019, September 4). Historic Beer Birthday: William Hamm, Jr. Retrieved May 18, 2020, from https://brookstonbeerbulletin.com/historic-beer-birthday-william-hamm-jr/

Browder, L. (2009). *Her Best Shot: Women and Guns in America*. UNC Press Books.

Caldwell, B. (2018, October 13). Barker gang made crime the family business. Retrieved May 18, 2020, from https://www.joplinglobe.com/news/local_news/bill-caldwell-barker-gang-made-crime-the-family-business/article_f4aebb31-afcb-5b71-b25c-dba37827ba7c.html

Callahan, J. (2016, December 25). Signet ring of notorius gangster found at Ocklawaha shootout site. Retrieved May 18, 2020, from https://www.ocala.com/news/20161225/signet-ring-of-notorius-gangster-found-at-ocklawaha-shootout-site

Chermak, S., & Bailey, F. Y. (2016). *Crimes of the Centuries: Notorious Crimes, Criminals, and Criminal Trials in American History [3 volumes]: Notorious Crimes, Criminals, and Criminal Trials in American History*. ABC-CLIO.

Clark, J., & Palattella, E. (2015). *A History of Heists: Bank Robbery in America*. Rowman & Littlefield.

Dill, E. (2019, November 15). Barker–Karpis Gang. Retrieved May 18, 2020, from https://www.mnopedia.org/group/barker-karpis-gang

Eddy, C. (2015, August 19). The Terrible Rise (and Subsequent Spectacular Fall) of the Barker/Karpis Gang. Retrieved May 18, 2020, from https://gizmodo.com/the-terrible-rise-and-subsequent-spectacular-fall-of-1725070298

Editors, A. Z. (2018). Alvin Karpis. Retrieved May 18, 2020, from https://www.alcatrazhistory.com/karpis.htm

Editors, B. C. (2020, May 11). Ma Barker Biography. Retrieved May 18, 2020, from https://www.biography.com/crime-figure/ma-barker

Editors, C. L. (2007, January 28). ALVIN KARPIS: PURSUIT OF THE LAST PUBLIC ENEMY. Retrieved May 18, 2020, from https://web.archive.org/web/20070128021941/http://www.crimelibrary.com/gangsters_outlaws/outlaws/karpis/1.html

Editors, C. E. (2017, August 6). Gangster Undressed. Retrieved May 18, 2020, from https://capturedandexposed.com/tag/lawrence-devol/

Editors, E. C. (2020, April 30). Barker, Ma (1872–1935). Retrieved May 18, 2020, from https://www.encyclopedia.com/women/encyclopedias-almanacs-transcripts-and-maps/barker-ma-1872-1935

Editors, F. B. (1936, November 19). THE KIDNAPING OF EDWARD GEORGE BREMER, ST. PAUL, MINNESOTA. . Retrieved May 18, 2AD, from https://static1.squarespace.com/static/54dc6b0be4b0d364a5ee20e0/t/596f525c893fc01a296bd706/1500467836964/1936 Barker:Karpis Summary.pdf

Editors, F. B. (2003, September 8). Latent Prints in the 1933 Hamm Kidnapping. Retrieved May 18, 2020, from https://archives.fbi.gov/archives/news/stories/2003/september/hamm090803

Editors, F. B. (2017). Barker/Karpis Gang. Retrieved May 18, 2020, from https://www.fbi.gov/history/famous-cases/barker-karpis-gang

Editors, F. B. (2017). Arthur R. "Doc" Barker Part 01 of 02. Retrieved May 18, 2020, from https://vault.fbi.gov/arthur-r.-doc-barker/arthur-r.-doc-barker-part-01-of-02/view

Editors, F. B. (2018). Kansas City Massacre/"Pretty Boy" Floyd. Retrieved May 18, 2020, from https://www.fbi.gov/history/famous-cases/kansas-city-massacre-pretty-boy-floyd

Editors, F. P. (2019, November 28). Ma Barker Biography. Retrieved May 18, 2020, from https://www.thefamouspeople.com/profiles/ma-barker-31417.php

Editors, H. C. (2009, November 13). Doc Barker is killed by prison guards as he attempts to escape. Retrieved May 18, 2020, from https://www.history.com/this-day-in-history/doc-barker-is-killed-by-prison-guards-as-he-attempts-to-escape

Editors, H. C. (2009, November 16). The Dalton Gang is wiped out in Coffeyville, Kansas. Retrieved May 18, 2020, from https://www.history.com/this-day-in-history/the-dalton-gang-is-wiped-out-in-coffeyville-kansas

Editors, H. B. (2013, April 9). THE FIRST NATIONAL OF FAIRBURY GETS HIT. Retrieved May 18, 2020, from http://homebrewedmojo.blogspot.com/2013/04/the-first-national-of-fairbury-gets-hit.html

Editors, H. B. (2017, May 12). THE BARKER-KARPIS DEAD. Retrieved May 18, 2020, from http://homebrewedmojo.blogspot.com/2017/05/the-barker-karpis-dead.html

Editors, H. G. (2017). THE BARKER/KARPIS GANG IN GENERAL. Retrieved May 18, 2020, from http://historicalgmen.squarespace.com/fbi-shooting-fred-kate-ma-b

Editors, H. B. (2017, April 25). MA'S MAN GETS MURDERED. Retrieved May 18, 2020, from http://homebrewedmojo.blogspot.com/2017/04/mas-man-gets-murdered.html

Editors, H. C. (2019, July 27). The Barker clan kills an officer in their fruitless robbery. Retrieved May 18, 2020, from https://www.history.com/this-day-in-history/the-barker-clan-kills-an-officer-in-their-fruitless-robbery

Editors, I. L. (2011, January 24). Barker Gang Has Ties To Local Town And Death Of Police Chief. Retrieved May 18, 2020, from http://www.imbodenlive.com/2011/01/24/barker-gang-has-ties-to-local-town-and-death-of-police-chief/

Editors, I. L. (2012, August 1). Unclaimed Safety Deposit Box In Pocahontas Opened 69 Years After Owner's Death Has Ties To Barker Gang. Retrieved May 18, 2020, from http://www.imbodenlive.com/2012/08/01/unclaimed-safety-deposit-box-in-pocahontas-opened-69-years-after-owners-death-has-ties-to-barker-gang/

Editors, J. S. (2016, February 22). Barker gang. Retrieved May 18, 2020, from https://journalstar.com/news/local/crime-and-courts/barker-gang/image_97856f69-7d98-5a2a-a0fc-ca80781e2687.html

Editors, K. T. (2020, January 17). Flashback Friday: Violent Midwest gang kidnaps St. Paul bank president for $200,000 ransom in 1934. Retrieved May 18, 2020, from https://kstp.com/news/flashback-friday-violent-midwest-gang-kidnapped-st-paul-bank-president-for-200k-in-ransom-money-in-1934/5607837/

Editors, M. F. (2004). Wynona Burdett and the FBI file: Barker-Karpis Gang. Retrieved May 18, 2020, from http://www.angelfire.com/mo3/mullenfamily/wynona2.html

Editors, M. B. (2015). The Ma Barker Story. Retrieved May 18, 2020, from https://mabarkerhouse.org/the-gang/

Editors, N. (1936). Bullets of Justice. Retrieved May 18, 2020, from https://www.newspapers.com/clip/28296157/kate-barker-ma-barker-1936-death/

Editors, O. P. (2016, October 27). Infamous 'Ma' Barker house crossed Lake Weir via barge. Retrieved May 18, 2020, from https://www.ocalapost.com/infamous-ma-barker-house-crossed-lake-weir-via-barge/

Editors, P. P. (2017). MA BARKER: MOTHER OF SEVERAL CRIMINALS WHO RAN THE BARKER GANG. Retrieved May 18, 2020, from https://peoplepill.com/people/ma-barker/

Editors, P. F. (2020). Leo R. Gorski. Retrieved May 18, 2020, from https://www.mpdfederation.com/leo-r-gorski/

Editors, T. O. (2007, December 30). Recalling a forgotten outlaw. Retrieved May 18, 2020, from https://oklahoman.com/article/3186836/recalling-a-forgotten-outlaw

Editors, W. S. (2017). Shootout With the "Ma" Barker Gang - Death of Sheriff Kelly. Retrieved May 18, 2020, from http://www.watersheds.org/education/richards/shootout.htm

Editors, W. (2019, September 19). Volney Davis. Retrieved May 18, 2020, from https://en.wikipedia.org/wiki/Volney_Davis

Editors, W. (2019, October 28). Lawrence DeVol. Retrieved May 18, 2020, from https://en.wikipedia.org/wiki/Lawrence_DeVol

Editors, W. D. (2019, February 28). Throwback Thursday: Car spotted in Lewiston may have been involved in Bremer kidnapping. Retrieved May 18, 2020,

from
https://www.winonadailynews.com/news/local/throwback
-thursday-car-spotted-in-lewiston-may-have-been-
involved/article_fd10111a-a8ff-56a0-8ed6-
b90ef86a4969.html

Editors, W. (2020, May 14). Alvin Karpis: Early Life.
Retrieved May 18, 2020, from
https://en.wikipedia.org/wiki/Alvin_Karpis#Early_life

Editors, Z. M. (2014, March). Matriarch Of Crime: Ma
Barker & the Barker Gang. Retrieved May 18, 2020, from
https://www.zmanmagazine.com/PDF/Z51 Ma Barker.pdf

Enns, C., & Kazanjian, H. (2016). *Ma Barker: America's
Most Wanted Mother*. Rowman & Littlefield.

Farris, D. (2016, August 11). A 1930s gang on the move
& involved in crime. Retrieved May 18, 2020, from
http://edmondlifeandleisure.com/a-s-gang-on-the-move-
involved-in-crime-p13220-76.htm

Farris, D. (2016, September 22). The Bremer
kidnapping. Retrieved May 18, 2020, from
http://edmondlifeandleisure.com/the-bremer-kidnapping-
p13433-76.htm

Frasca, M. A. (2015). *Mafia Hits: 100 Murders that
changed the Mob*. Arcturus Publishing.

Gerkin, S. (2011, July 6). THE REIGN OF CREEPY. Retrieved May 18, 2020, from https://thislandpress.com/2011/07/06/creepy-karpis-and-the-tulsa-central-park-gang/

Gorny, N. (2016, August 7). More Ma Barker: Family stories highlight local interactions. Retrieved May 18, 2020, from https://www.ocala.com/news/20160807/more-ma-barker-family-stories-highlight-local-interactions

Guthrey, M. (2017, May 27). Ma Barker gang's old West St. Paul hideout for sale. Retrieved May 18, 2020, from https://www.twincities.com/2017/05/27/depression-era-gangsters-lair-for-sale-in-west-st-paul/

Hunt, B. (2016, February 28). DOC BARKER'S LAST ESCAPE. Retrieved May 18, 2020, from https://bhunt34.wordpress.com/2016/02/28/doc-barkers-last-escape/

Krehbiel, R., & Jackson, D. (2016, December 17). Notorious Tulsa — 12 crime stories from Tulsa's past. Retrieved May 18, 2020, from https://www.tulsaworld.com/lifestyles/magazine/notorious-tulsa-12-crime-stories-from-tulsas-past/article_af8f0168-8ce0-5a55-bf5d-3a0dc222259e.html

McCabe, S. (2012, January 12). Crime History: Doc Barker killed trying to escape Alcatraz. Retrieved May 18,

2020, from https://www.washingtonexaminer.com/crime-history-doc-barker-killed-trying-to-escape-alcatraz

Munro, A. (2014, June 9). Ma Barker. Retrieved May 18, 2020, from https://www.britannica.com/biography/Ma-Barker

O'Dell, L. (2010). BARKER GANG. Retrieved May 18, 2020, from https://www.okhistory.org/publications/enc/entry.php?entry=BA038

O'Neill, N. (2016, October 28). Ma Barker isn't happy about her house being moved. Retrieved May 18, 2020, from https://nypost.com/2016/10/28/ma-barker-isnt-happy-about-her-house-being-moved/

Peck, L. (2016, June). Abducted in St. Paul! Retrieved May 18, 2020, from https://www.minnesotagoodage.com/voices/mn-history/2016/06/abducted-in-st-paul/

Reeves, B. (2016, November 16). A Hamm's ransom: How the kidnapping of one of St. Paul's most prosperous brewers reshaped a corrupt system. Retrieved May 18, 2020, from https://growlermag.com/a-hamms-ransom-how-the-kidnapping-of-one-of-st-pauls-most-prosperous-brewers-reshaped-a-corrupt-system/

Rubin, B. P. (2015, April 22). The Forgotten Crime Boss: Kid Cann, the Original Teflon Don, Reigned Over Minneapolis. Retrieved May 18, 2020, from http://www.citypages.com/news/the-forgotten-crime-boss-kid-cann-the-original-teflon-don-reigned-over-minneapolis-6570344

Skousen, W. C. (2014). *True Stories from the Files of the Fbi*. Izzard Ink.

Smith, R. B. (2013). *Outlaw Tales of Oklahoma: True Stories of the Sooner State's Most Infamous Crooks, Culprits, and Cutthroats*. Rowman & Littlefield.

Smyth, M. (1986, October 19). TOWN WHERE MA BARKER DIED SURE THAT ALLIGATOR DID HER IN. Retrieved May 18, 2020, from https://www.chicagotribune.com/news/ct-xpm-1986-10-19-8603190027-story.html

Stewart, T. (2018). *Ma Barker In Ocklawaha*. Lulu.com.

Taylor, T. (2015, January 16). THE LAST GREAT OUTLAW GANG. Retrieved May 18, 2020, from http://troytaylorbooks.blogspot.com/2015/01/the-last-great-outlaw-gang.html

Tippet, P. (2013). Edna Murray: The Kissing Bandit. Retrieved May 18, 2020, from http://pamtippet.com/ednamurray/edna_pg1.html

Walker, W. (2018, January 23). Barker-Karpis Gang. Retrieved May 18, 2020, from https://encyclopediaofarkansas.net/entries/barker-karpis-gang-5740/

Weiser-Alexander, K. (2018, November). Barker-Karpis Gang – Terrorizing the Midwest. Retrieved May 18, 2020, from https://www.legendsofamerica.com/barker-karpis/

Weiser-Alexander, K. (2018, November). Arthur R. "Doc" Barker – Killed at Alcatraz. Retrieved May 18, 2020, from https://www.legendsofamerica.com/doc-barker/

Weiser-Alexander, K. (2020, January). Edna Murray – The Kissing Bandit. Retrieved May 18, 2020, from https://www.legendsofamerica.com/edna-murray/

Weiser-Alexander, K. (2020, January). Joseph P. Moran – Gangster Doctor. Retrieved May 18, 2020, from https://www.legendsofamerica.com/joseph-moran/

White, C. (2018, September 21). LEAVE NO TRACE. Retrieved May 18, 2020, from https://themobmuseum.org/blog/leave-no-trace/

Wood, L. (2015, October 16). It's All in the Past: The Barker Gang and the murder of Sheriff Kelly. Retrieved May 18, 2020, from https://www.therolladailynews.com/article/20151016/NE

Wood, L. (2015, October 17). The Barker Gang and the murder of Sheriff Kelly. Retrieved May 18, 2020, from https://dailyjournalonline.com/news/the-barker-gang-and-the-murder-of-sheriff-kelly/article_19b62a7f-f301-52d1-bcab-a2d5d9bcc561.html

Free Books by Charles River Editors

We have brand new titles available for free most days of the week. To see which of our titles are currently free, click on this link.

Discounted Books by Charles River Editors

We have titles at a discount price of just 99 cents everyday. To see which of our titles are currently 99 cents, click on this link.